At Creation's Open Door

*For Sherry
 who already knows
 about the pain
 and ecstasy of writing.*

Eleanor Fitzgibbons

At Creation's Open Door

Eleanor Fitzgibbons, IHM

Scythe Publications, Inc.
A Division of Winston-Derek Publishers Group, Inc.

The author gratefully acknowledges the following publications in which some of these poems first appeared:

The Archer, Christian Century, Commonweal, Contact, Groundwork, Jonah's Wail, Review for Religious, Sisters Today, Sparrow, Spirited Words, Stirrings.

© 1995 by Eleanor Fitzgibbons

All rights reserved. No part of this book may be reproduced in any form without written permission from the publishers, except by a reviewer who may quote brief passages in a review to be printed in a newspaper or magazine.

First printing

Cover Design by June Steckler

PUBLISHED BY SCYTHE PUBLICATIONS, INC.
Nashville, Tennessee 37205

Library of Congress Catalog Card No: 93-60358
ISBN: 1-55523-622-7

Printed in the United States of America

*To the Poet of poets
Who has created us
for immortal beauty*

Contents

Part I
The Miracle of Seeing

1 Dreamland
2 Morning Praise
3 Love Song
4 Dandelions
5 The River Wife
6 Anniversary
7 Silent Music
8 The Hawk
9 My Sister the Tulip Tree
10 Common Denominator
11 Night Bird
12 Partners
13 Waiting for the Verdict
14 Hospital Trilogy
16 Peonies for Remembrance
17 Pastorale
18 Early Childhood Education

Part II
The Color and Shape of Love

20 O Wondrous Mystery
21 The Moment of Christmas
22 Texas Christmas
23 Mother of God
24 Lord of the Temple
25 Parable
26 The Reign of God
27 Ocean Resort on Good Friday
28 Winter Triptych
30 Good Friday
31 Talitha Cumi

Part III
"All shall be well."

35 From My Hermitage
36 On My Birthday
37 Before I Knew You
38 Invitation
39 Recommitment
40 Psalm for a Summer Day
41 My Beloved
42 Lord of Sciatica
43 Hundredfold
44 Magnificat

Part IV
A Carousel of Seasons

46 Spring Tonic
47 After April Rain
48 Butterfly Debut
49 Drought
50 Secrets
51 Helpless
52 Flashback
53 Elegy
54 October
55 Transfiguration
56 Providence
57 Li Po's Winter Eyes

Part V
When Poetry Is Calling

61 Rumblings Against the Night
62 At a Trident Missile Base
63 Mothers of the Plaza
64 To a Poet
65 Pigeon Wisdom
66 The Way of a Poem

Part I

The Miracle of Seeing

Dreamland

Home for me, a noisy metropolis
where gray days outnumber sun
six to one sometimes.

No wonder this lush tropical island
made me think of the original Eve
waking to Paradise.

Now God had created the earth
all over again. I too looked out on Eden
and pronounced it good.

Royal palms gloriously crowned,
sun-flecked, blue-green sea;
long wide beaches, snow-white sand.

On pilings in the bay
snowy egret, pelican
perched side by side.

Time slips out of its frenzy.
I wake and sleep to the music of water
lapping the sides of sailboat
lying at anchor.

Who would imagine a place like this for grief?

Morning Praise

Mostly anonymous
worshippers:

dandelions
in ballerina skirts
polka dotting acres
of dancing green

chee chee cheeing
robins nesting
fussy as a mother hen

a cardinal
madly darting for seeds

in between his piercingly
exquisite wooing of
Marie! Marie! Marie!

How his dashing redemptive red
sends new blood racing
through tired winter veins!

God, meanwhile,
(so easily touched)
looking on and listening,
enormously pleased.

Love Song

Here
at the window
of Joy

I stand
tree-high

lighter
than milkweed silk

so close to sky
I could snatch a star
and set it spinning!

Dandelions

I hear a poet rhapsodize
over this daytime miracle:
green-gold starry skies.

The gardener (April's hard
on rheumatism) spits a curse
upon the "blasted weeds, confound them!"

Chains or diadem, dandelions
are what we make of them;
Dandelions (like love)
are what we see in them.

The River Wife

I heard whistling swans
last night
close by on the melting ice

but you were not here
beside me
listening in the dark
to the ushering in of spring.

It wasn't the same.

Anniversary

I went seeking
a witness-sign
to confirm my morning pledge.

Timeless, winterwise
Love pointed beyond
a summer hedge to

Asters
spangling dry earth
constant with stars;

Chrysanthemums
sustaining hoarfrost,
snow.

Silent Music

Close to the stage
in the darkened symphony hall

I'm one with the tempestuous music
of Beethoven's "Appassionata"

until
I see the white moth—
a winged ballerina

fluttering out of the shadows
mesmerized by the lights.

Up center stage
it floats and gyrates

soars and plunges with the music
"appassionata"

Now it leaps and stays
poised in mid-air

like a hummingbird
in motionless motion

alone
in the blinding darkness
of light.

Suddenly
it darts upward again
in utter ecstasy

closer
mounting closer
irresistibly drawn

to the waiting moon of fire.

"For love is like fire which ever rises upward with the desire to be absorbed in the center of its sphere."   St. John of the Cross

The Hawk

With what careless freedom O
how you sweep and careen
in the blue morning sky

higher, higher O
to what altitudes of ecstasy you soar
clearing mountains of cloud

on a breeze of abandon and lightness O
how you dare with the brashness of Icarus
to penetrate higher air

closing in on sun itself
until I cannot face the glare
and shade my eyes while

you and the light are one.

My Sister the Tulip Tree

stands
tall
slender
in gold brocade

against a tapestry
of woods in flowing
burgundy, crimson, ocher, brown.

Graceful,
graciously unaware,

You stir us
if ever so briefly
into seeing how

Beauty always
all ways is
its own excuse for being.

Common Denominator

A wisp of white-haired woman
Stops me on the street.

Lonely, she tells me,
So alone

She would share with me,
A Gentile,

Her kosher kitchen
If I needed a place.
Why not?

"People is people."

Night Bird

Night bird flying low
at the end of a lavender sky

into the silent implacable dark

No olive branch to break your flight
No waiting ark.

Partners

So, I was not the only one
in dire trouble, buffeted by

winds of contradiction, tempted
to give up the struggle.

You too were having a bad time,
tree outside my window,

I can tell by all the broken
branches, twigs violently
snapped and scattered.

What dark wind-angel
did you wrestle with last night
for a precious Jacob-blessing?

Waiting for the Verdict

X-rays, biopsy over, now you wait
exquisitely aware of your taken-for-granted
creaturely self:

the soothing rhythm of every moment's breath
and reassuring feel of smooth warm flesh;

taste of salt on nervous lips, that
delicate shell of sound, your ear;

the miracle of seeing—mind's vast
hemispheres, imagination's boundless arc,

but god-like, most astounding gift—
the human heart. You let tears fall.

Long ago, a Latin poet sang about
"lacrimae rerum"—the "tears of things."

O rainbow freshness look
of never-seen-before, as if with Adam

you were standing for the first time
at creation's open door

breathless, wonderstruck—alive!

Hospital Trilogy

I

My roommate, victim of a recent stroke,
Naomi, many years a wife

For the first time helpless in a strange and narrow bed,

Her quick mind apt to fail her now
without a moment's warning.

"What do you give up,"
she asks a nurse
"in order to be near your husband?"

"What do you mean, Naomi?"

Silence—blank—all the hunger
loneliness, desire gone.

A sphinx stares out
from a frame of crumpled pillow.

II

Morning—
"Are you awake, Naomi?" I whisper.

"Not really," she replies.

I mourn the unwitting truth
in her response.

No, I do not want to read
the writing on Naomi's wall.

I do not want to diagram
the hard syntax of her present-future,

Define, make clear her painful verbs:
I was . . . I am
I will be . . .

III

Husband Dan shows me a photo of
Naomi dancing at their grandson's wedding
two short months ago—

Naomi, lightly on her toes and laughing
clapping a folk dance with partner Ruth,
her favorite daughter-in-law.

How little did they know that day,
Naomi and Ruth—

How little do we know!

Peonies for Remembrance
In Memoriam J.G.F.

Peonies—
a favorite from early childhood

when you and I stood
head to head with them,
breathing in their heady fragrance,

amused at feverish ants
working the scented paths
    up
    down
    in
    out
round and round
labyrinthine petals.

Today,
years and thousands of miles later
I came upon a painted sea-green vase
lush with pink and white
"Peonies by Picasso."

Instantly,
a recent grief remembered:

the anxious night-call,
my hurried flight in the foreboding
dark of a lingering winter.

Our loss and grieving . . .
the comforting of friends and

unexpected solace of sunlight
warming a new niche
in the gray stone of a columbarium

wind and waves close by
washing the sea-walls of a lake we loved,
my brother and I.

Pastorale
(*for Irene*)

The air is so pure here
I can see where sky touches down
on green seas of wheat in the morning sun.

Listen to that thrush
in the flowering crab apple

And look, a butterfly flitting
around the lilacs, among the peonies
in the wisteria . . .

How you would run after those
winged marvels when we were children,
such cries of delight
yet never catching one . . .

And then later, in the troubled years later,
your never ended reaching after
the peace always eluding your heart.

Peace.
A wind sighs in the willow . . .
Peace, Dear Heart.

Early Childhood Education

She was our near neighbor—childless
And I was always welcome, lured
By cookies and attention.

Did I help to fill her hunger?
She was good for me, I know,
Until that afternoon when
He came home and they quarreled
As if I were not there,

Too young to understand how
People can hate and love each other
With such single-hearted passion—

But there I was—transfixed
Between two raging fires.

How glad at last to slip away
And run home in time for dinner
Where the Tiffany lamp
Shed a soothing glow and
It was peaceful at our table.

Why so quiet? they wanted to know
But I could not break the ice
That held it captive—
My terrible secret trouble.

Part II

The Color and Shape of Love

O Wondrous Mystery

Under world's largest dome
the starlit heavens

ever so quietly
He left his home

to pitch his tent
among us

tent
of his bones and body

God-made-flesh to be
like one of us.

But as to the tent
of his dwelling-place:

unlike the rest of us
he was born in a cave

and died on a cross
like a low-down knave

all for love of us

but betwixt and between
there came a day

when his heart was so full
he was heard to say:

Foxes have holes . . .
Birds in the air their nests

But the Son of Man
has nowhere to rest
nowhere to lay his head.

The Moment of Christmas

Past anguish—all forgotten
Future—in the future
Present—unchecked joy

If walls and floor are dusty
And oil lamp is sputtering

If cave is cold and musty
And tethered dozing donkey
Is having a mulish dream

If shepherds, on word of angels,
And magi from afar are setting out
To worship guided by a star

At the moment it does not matter
As Mary's newborn Miracle
is cradled on her breast.

Texas Christmas

Inside the house
A snow-flecked tree
Adazzle with flowing pendants—

Birds and angels
Singing in silent praise.

Outside the house
A magnolia tree
Lit up with a maze of finches—

Winged magi
Bringing gold from the North

Singing in bird-tongues of praise
To the Word made Flesh

In the wordless Infant
Asleep in a manger on hay.

Mother of God
(Vladimir Madonna, Byzantine Icon, 12th century)

The child has been frightened
Right out of his divinity.

What sudden terror or harrowing dream
Foreshadowing great harm
Has sent him running to sanctuary
In the safety of her arms?

Powerless to shield, forestall
The passion of what bitter hour.

His face upturned for comfort
Meets the pain her eyes convey
Of birth and flight, peril, sword,
And prophecy that will not go away.

Lord of the Temple

Wind-raw and stubble-patch:
unlikely road to revelation
on a winter Sunday morning.

And then,
I came upon a field of wheat
green as fresh cut grass!

Who broke the letter of the law
and brought this miracle of spring to pass
in stark December?

and I remembered
a man
whose hungry disciples plucked ears of grain
on the Sabbath.

Parable

The kingdom of God is like
a flowering cottonwood tree

when it drops its downy seeds
filling the air with clouds
of floating fleur-de-lis.

Some fall on sterile pavement
soon crushed under foot and wheel—

Others, intercepted,
are caught in prickly hedges
fruition stayed—

And many drift down
on the sandy roadside,
long ribbons of yellowing cotton
to be swept and thrown away—

But others find rest
in fertile spaces to yield

Who knows how many trees?

The Reign of God
"Like mustard seed . . . a pearl." (Matt. 13)

I found the kingdom of God last night
At a wedding banquet with friends.

No last or first at table,
No marks of power, place—

Waiters danced with the bride and her guests,
The cook and her staff with the groom.

A midget stepped out for every dance
And she never danced alone.

I found the kingdom of God last night
In the color and shape of love.

Ocean Resort on Good Friday

The business of work and pleasure
Per usual
From noon till three today.

What happened two thousand years ago?

Yachts and their merry riders
Empty the lush marina.

Down on the clubhouse lawn
A woman stretched in the sun,
Crucifying her flesh
For the sake of a tan.

Pounding of hammers and nails
On a rising condo across the canal.

Pop . . . puff . . . pop
On the tennis court.
Someone calls "Love!"

What is love?

Today, Good Friday,
Money is king on the beach.

Who remembers the price of betrayal?

Even the sun has forgotten
Not to shine.

Winter Triptych
Outdoor Stations of the Cross

Tenth Station
Jesus is stripped of his clothing

Not in this snowfall.

Mary's Son
stands
fully robed
in
compassionate
white.

Twelfth Station
Jesus dies on the cross

"It is finished."

A spider has drawn
her silken veil over

the closed and
swollen eyes.

Thank you, Veronica.

Thirteenth Station
Jesus is taken down from the cross

From a distance
it looks like a miniature chalet
flanked by fir trees
in the snow

A peaceful outdoor crèche

But here, no angel's word
no star
no heavenly song

to comfort this desolate mother
mourning the dead son
on her knees.

Good Friday
(. . . *pierced through for us all* . . . Isaiah)

An old wooden crucifix

one crossbeam
warped

leans forward

any moment
to leap
down
from high wall.

This eager Christ
cannot wait
three long hours more

so passionately
wanting
our fall back
into grace.

Talitha Cumi
("Little girl, arise!" Matt. 9:18)

Joy
can be sudden too,
unpredictable as pain.

From the dark roots of death
it blossoms at a word

and sets the daughter of Jairus
dancing!

Part III

"All shall be well."

From My Hermitage

a wilderness
of trees

lights up
with rapture

when God appears
in sunrise.

On My Birthday

God of Surprises!

You reveal yourself
in a hazel nut:

"Look, I tell you,
All shall be well.
I can, I shall, I make
all things well."

You house yourself
in a barnacle
no storm can budge
from the shell of a conch,

a symbol, I'd say,
of yourself—determined
inveterate lover.

And now today
on my birthday

heaven itself falls down.
You come disguised
in an ocean of fog.

Unafraid, I float,
rising and falling
with the billows—

I know you are here
in the darkness

Shining invisible Swimmer

Strong arms upholding me,
the silence quivering with love.

Before I Knew You

in the freedom of Wind and Fire,

how often
You were the lonely one

waiting   unseen   unheard

that phantom false god
blocking my door

the One-Eyed Book Keeper
who taught me fear.

II

And so
in what panic and longing

I fled my house
looking in blind alleys

restless   empty   unsatisfied

while all the while
in the glowing spark

You were with me, Love,
right here at home.

Invitation

Today,
Sky, dove-simple
Total gray.

Are You saying

Now is the moment,
Come, turn away

To the still point of
Your heart's deep center.

There in the darkness of
My healing light

You will see
Mirages of desire disappear

Dazzling pebbles
In semblance of the Pearl.

I will fill your hunger
With my love

Make you content
With nothing less.

Recommitment

The dogwood tree
outside the College Chapel
has flowered again.

Everywhere
its flame-tipped petals
have fallen and scattered like stars

in the chinks of weathered sidewalk,
over the lawn,

on the road to the library
where tires press them into poems
on the pages of summer.

The dogwood tree has flowered
and showered its gift
in clouds of bright abandon.

It does not know circumspection
thrift, delay.

The great white dogwood bloom
stirs petals in my mind.

I open all my windows
to give the Spirit room.

Psalm for a Summer Day

As tiger lilies
open and turn
toward the morning sun

so do I wake to you, my God,
so do I thirst after you
the living water.

My Beloved

is in the cool
morning breeze

that runs like
a fresh current

through the drowsy
leaves of woods

waking after
a sultry night.

Lord of Sciatica

Why not?

You who calmed your quaking disciples,
Seasoned sailors all—
You who commanded the hell-bent winds
On a raging sea to be still—

You who cherish each hair on our heads
And remind us
How much we are more than the sparrows
You feed and note every fall—

Can you not restrain an unruly nerve
From crippling the body you made?
O God of our wholeness and faithful lover,
Why not?

Hundredfold

The soul has
nights of cold
and desert days.

It's then He sends her
John,

not the Baptist clad
in camel's hair

to warn
of coming wrath
and casting into fire,

but
John he sends
who leaned upon his breast.

Magnificat

Out of your tender mercies, my God,
I lovingly lift up the years.

Child in me claps and dances,
Joy in the woman breaks soundless
Too deep for laughter or tears.

I flounder for words to thank you
And offer my silence for song.

Part IV

A Carousel of Seasons

Spring Tonic

Impatiently
I headed toward the back fence—

Paper litter again!

But stood
totally disarmed instead
before the radiant offenders:

A patch of snow-white trillium.

After April Rain

Sun sets:

a luminous
pearl

in clam-shell
sky

Butterfly Debut

Mid-morning a chrysalis opens:

    Regal Frittilary
stirs from her silken sleep
        her wings to dry

      to blue velvet
        mother-of-pearl   burnished silver

        into sunlight
fit for a queen.

Drought

The stricken trees are psalms of desolation
Pleading and lamenting on their plight.

Parched root and withered leaves cry to the God
of their summer growth and greening:

How can we wave branches of praise before you?
Be glad Hosannas in this crackling grist of dry

Tormented land, earth where no water is, only
Mocking skies and angry sun.

Will you who made us let your beauty perish?
Speak, we implore, the healing word of *rain*.

Secrets

The wind is saying something
to the trees.

They are jubilant, ecstatic,
Branches swaying, bowing,
Transfigured in the sun.

Yes, oh yes, touch us, tell us
over and over!

Leaves trembling to the greenest tip,
Branches bending to hear—

What is wind sharing with the trees?

Helpless

I watch
the kiss of death

repeated
relentlessly

branch
on
branch

limb
after
limb

up
up
to the topmost
leaf

of my
tulip tree.

Flashback

From my window I followed
a golden butterfly
zigzagging this way and that
in the sweet summer air—

It fluttered and paused
on a lilac branch, then away
to another and still another

Up and down, here and there
without apparent purpose—
there were no flowers,
lilac season was over—

I saw no reason
for this endless flitting
'til it suddenly fluttered
around the corner and out of view

When just as abruptly
I remembered why
someone once called me a
butterfly.

Elegy

Could wood mourn
we'd hear
loud
lamenting
for the oak
that did not
stand the storm.

October

The wren house
empty now:
deserted red pagoda
in the Chinese maple.

Transfiguration

I did not have to
climb a mountain

go further than my door

to see a leafless oak tree
light up in glory

branch after branch
take flame and soar.

Providence

Let maples take a crimson turn and
Robins are winging southward
Safe from hazards of winter season.

But willy-nilly, come what may:
Ice storms, blizzard, Saharas of snow—
Sparrows stay.

It's true—they have not sown
Or reaped or stashed any silos with
Seed for the winter—

Yet somehow they know
Someone will feed them.

Li Po's Winter Eyes

Mourning doves
line bare branches:

motionless Buddhas
in the winter sun

Ghost
of meadow lark
on dry stalk

of milkweed
in December

Under a light snow screen
leaves on the driveway
glistening in the sun:

fallen star shells

Hurry, look!
Sun is cutting diamonds
all over the snow

Tilting mast
of a shipwreck
sinking in the snow:

Young birch tree
bending in the blizzard

Uh oh!
Mourning dove mating call
in this freak January
April Fool spring weather

Part V

When Poetry Is Calling

Rumblings Against the Night

An angry jay
in the mountain ash

impotent to rout
trespassing crows—

On my desk
a withered branch
of burning bush

each wizened berry
a grinning skull

the progeny
of summer drought—

This small familiar
place called "home"

a microcosmic hull
of inner/outer space.

For all its surface loveliness
Earth grieves and sickens
lacking love—

In broad daylight
her killer walks:

Greed poisons plant and tree and air
Greed stalks our skies and waters

Sowing blight.

At a Trident Missile Base

Holding his infant daughter
A peacemaker crosses the line
into the arsenal that cradles
Warheads, nuclear arms.

"They will bring bazookas,"
the townfolk muttered.
(The business of weapons had
become daily bread buttered.)

"Tell them," he whispered,
"We brought babies."

Mothers of the Plaza

Undeterred by flailing clubs
by tear and vomit gas or worse,

their own lives imperilled, yet
every week they come to the plaza

faithful to the search for those
who have been taken from them.

Their silence rises in deafening waves
crying on the Powers
to tell the truth about their men:

husband, father, brother, son—
The Disappeared.

These resolute women
lack even the terrible comfort
of Mary's certainty

Mother most sorrowful
holding her murdered son
at the foot of the torture tree.

To a Poet

Tongue-tied by joy
I listen to you
reading your poems
and bringing me
to life in them.

You cannot see

the bright phoenix
from its ashes rising
on the dark skies
of my silence

or the flowers
opening in the rain
on my desert sands.

Pigeon Wisdom

From my carrel window in the library stacks
I watch five city pigeons

on the sun-baked parking lot
picking, pecking, pecking, picking—

What does barren cement have to offer them
with fresh green grass only five yards away?

But more to the point—

Why let dull pigeon-folly distract me
when Poetry is calling from Parnassus
between the covers of my waiting book!

The Way of a Poem

It comes
innocently at first—
the unexpected insight or phrase
begging a little consideration
at your imagination's door—

Then
growing bolder word by word
it forces entrance with a passion
that defies expulsion
demanding your undivided attention.

You love the labor
all protests to the contrary and
other obligations notwithstanding

until the finished poem
like Galatea—breathing—radiant
comes alive before you

and you pray it will happen again!